LIFE CYCLES
Grasshoppers

by Robin Nelson

first step nonfiction

Lerner Publications Company · Minneapolis

Look at the **grasshopper**.

There are many kinds of
grasshoppers.

A grasshopper is an **insect**, like a fly or an ant.

How does a grasshopper grow?

A female lays eggs in
the ground.

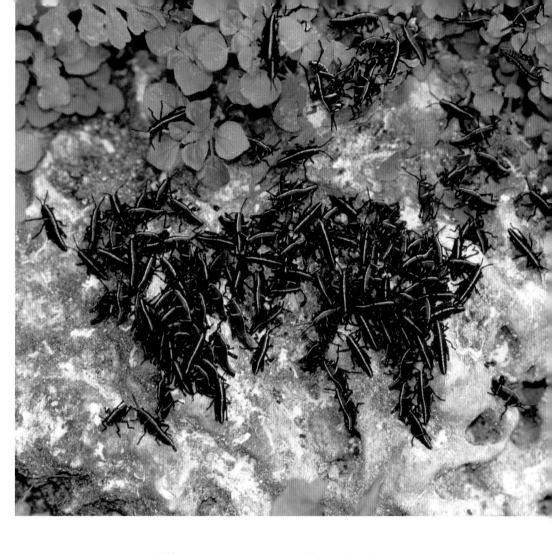

The eggs **hatch**.

Soon it is a **nymph**.

A nymph does not have wings.

The nymph eats a lot.

The nymph grows bigger
and bigger.

Nymphs have a hard shell covering their bodies.

The nymph **sheds** this shell
as it gets bigger.

Soon it is a grasshopper.

Adult grasshoppers have wings.

The grasshopper jumps
away.

It is fun to watch a
grasshopper grow.

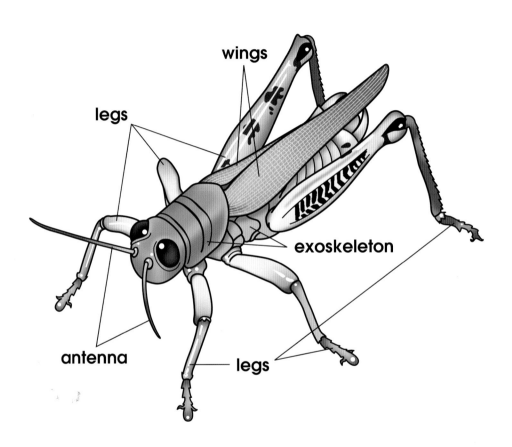

wings

legs

antenna

exoskeleton

legs

Adult Grasshoppers

Adult grasshoppers have strong back legs. These legs help them to jump far. Jumping keeps them safe from enemies like birds and other animals.

Female grasshoppers lay more than 100 eggs in the fall. In the spring, grasshopper eggs hatch, and a new grasshopper life cycle begins.

Grasshopper Facts

 The hard shell covering the grasshopper nymph's body is called an exoskeleton.

 When a grasshopper nymph sheds its exoskeleton, a new one forms. This is called molting.

 Grasshopper nymphs shed their exoskeletons five times before they become an adult.

 Grasshoppers can feel and smell with their antennas.

Male grasshoppers make a singing sound with their wings or legs.

There are about 10,000 different kinds of grasshoppers.

Grasshoppers are found all over the world except where it is very cold like near the North Pole and the South Pole.

Glossary

 grasshopper – an insect with wings and long legs for jumping

 hatch – to come out of an egg

 insect – an animal with six legs and three main body parts

 nymph – young insect

 sheds – drops or loses

Index

The images in this book are used with the permission of: © James Urbach/SuperStock, p. 2; © age fotostock/SuperStock, p. 3 (bottom right); © Gerry Lemmo, pp. 3 (both top, bottom left), 4; © Charles O. Slavens/Peter Arnold, Inc., p. 5; © Charles Melton/Visuals Unlimited, Inc., p. 6; © James H. Robinson/Photo Researchers, Inc., pp. 7, 13, 15, 22 (top, second from top, bottom); © David Kuhn/Dwight Kuhn Photography, pp. 8, 9, 10, 22 (second from bottom); © Gary Neil Corbett/SuperStock, p. 11; © Theo Allofs/The Image Bank/Getty Images, p. 12; © Luis Castaneda Inc./The Image Bank/Getty Images, pp. 14, 22 (middle); © Dwight Kuhn, p. 16; © Tamara Staples/The Image Bank/Getty Images, p. 17; © Laura Westlund/Independent Picture Service, p. 18.
Front Cover: © Luis Castaneda Inc./The Image Bank/Getty Images.

Lerner Publications Company
A division of Lerner Publishing Group, Inc.
241 First Avenue North
Minneapolis, MN 55401 U.S.A.

Website address: www.lernerbooks.com

Library of Congress Cataloging-in-Publication Data

Nelson, Robin, 1971–
        Grasshoppers / by Robin Nelson.
            p.   cm. — (First step nonfiction. Animal life cycles)
        Includes index.
        ISBN: 978–0–7613–4063–8 (lib. bdg. : alk. paper)
        1. Grasshoppers—Life cycles—Juvenile literature.
    I. Title.
    QL508.A2N45 2009
    595.7'26—dc22   2008029436

Manufactured in the United States of America
1 2 3 4 5 6 – DP – 14 13 12 11 10 09